THE
AMAZING
POTATO

Also by Milton Meltzer

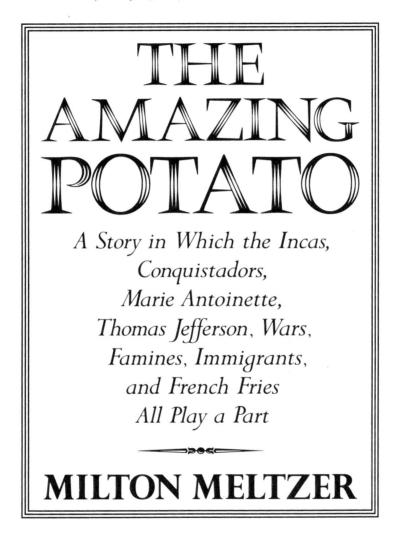

THE AMAZING POTATO

A Story in Which the Incas,
Conquistadors,
Marie Antoinette,
Thomas Jefferson, Wars,
Famines, Immigrants,
and French Fries
All Play a Part

MILTON MELTZER

HarperCollins*Publishers*

For the new Zachary

THE AMAZING POTATO
*A Story in Which the Incas, Conquistadors, Marie Antoinette, Thomas
Jefferson, Wars, Famines, Immigrants, and French Fries All Play a Part*

Copyright © 1992 by Milton Meltzer
All rights reserved. No part of this book may be used or
reproduced in any manner whatsoever without written
permission except in the case of brief quotations
embodied in critical articles and reviews.
Printed in the United States of America.
For information address HarperCollins Children's Books,
a division of HarperCollins Publishers,
10 East 53rd Street, New York, NY 10022.
Typography by Elynn Cohen
1 2 3 4 5 6 7 8 9 10
First Edition

Library of Congress Cataloging-in-Publication Data
Meltzer, Milton, date
    The amazing potato : a story in which the Incas, conquistadors,
Marie Antoinette, Thomas Jefferson, wars, famines, immigrants,
and french fries all play a part / by Milton Meltzer.
        p.   cm.
    Includes bibliographical references and index.
    Summary: Introduces the history, effects, and current uses of
the potato in the world marketplace.
    ISBN 0-06-020806-6. — ISBN 0-06-020807-4 (lib. bdg.)
    1. Potatoes—History—Juvenile literature.
2. Potatoes—Social aspects—Juvenile literature.
3. Potatoes—Juvenile literature.   [1.Potatoes.]
SB211.P8M53   1992   91-29610
 635' .21—dc20   CIP
                                                                AC

❧ *Acknowledgments* ❧

Every effort has been made to locate the copyright holders of all copyrighted materials and secure the necessary permission to reproduce them. In the event of any questions arising as to their use, the publisher will be glad to make changes in future printings and editions.

We gratefully acknowledge the Picture Collection of the New York Public Library as a resource for many of the illustrations in this book.

In addition, we acknowledge the following individuals, books, and institutions, the illustrations provided to us, and list the pages on which the illustrations appear:

Page 18: Potato Association of America, Orono, Maine. • Page 20: *The Route of the Incas*, by Hans Silvester and Jacques Soustelle. Copyright © 1977 by Thames & Hudson Ltd. for English language translation. Copyright © 1976 Hans Silvester (photographs), Jacques Soustelle (text). Used by permission of Viking Penguin, a division of Penguin Books USA Inc. • Page 21: United Nations, photo #33427. • Pages 28, 30 and 37: The Metropolitan Museum of Art: on page 28: Harris Brisbane Dick Fund, 1926 (26.48.6); on page 30: Mr. & Mrs. Isaac D. Fletcher Collection, Bequest of Isaac D. Fletcher, 1917 (17.120.119); on page 37: Bequest of Miss Adelaide Milton de Groot (1876–1967), 1967. • Page 41: Winfield Parks, © 1971 National Geographic Society. • Pages 51 and 59: State Historical Society of Wisconsin. • Pages 55, 64, and 65: The New-York Historical Society, New York City. • Page 58: National Park Service, Statue of Liberty National Monument. • Page 61: Museum of the City of New York; in *Harpers Weekly*, June 26, 1869. • Page 69: Harlan Logan. • Page 71: *The Complete Book of Fruits and Vegetables*, by Francesco Bianchini and Corbetta F. Bianchini, illustrated by Marilena Pistoria. Copyright © 1973 by Arnoldo Mondadori Editore Milano. Reprinted by permission of Crown Publishers, Inc. • Page 72: Agricultural Research Service. • Page 77: F.J. Koch. • Pages 83 and 84: U.S. Department of Agriculture; on page 83: Erwin W. Cole, photographer.

❧ Contents ❧

Foreword

One summer afternoon several years ago, browsing in a bookshop at Cambridge University, I noticed a fat brown paperback called *The History and Social Influence of the Potato*. I picked it up, wondering how anyone could write so big a book on so unlikely a subject. The potato! And nearly 700 closely printed pages of it! Dr. Redcliffe Salaman had spent a lifetime studying the potato in all the aspects the title suggests. The reviews quoted on the back cover called it "profound" and "noble" and "a magnificent monument of scholarship and humanity."

What could justify all those fine words? I bought a copy and carted it home from England. One evening, after long hours at my desk, I took it down from a shelf and dipped into the middle. The page was so packed with facts utterly new and startling to me, and insights so stimulating, I went back to the beginning and read it night after night till the end.

From that time on, whenever the word "potato" caught my eye in a newspaper or magazine or book, I scribbled a note and stowed it away. Then one morning as I woke, I knew I was going to write my own book about the potato for young readers. I wanted them to see how such an everyday object, one we scarcely ever notice except perhaps when we have a hankering for french fries, can be of such vast significance in the history of humankind.

—Milton Meltzer

Tons of Potatoes, Billions of Dollars

*J*ust the other day you walked into a McDonald's.

"Gimme a Big Mac!" you said.

"And potatoes?" asked the girl behind the counter.

"Yeah. Make it a large order of fries."

You picked up your tray, sat down at a table, and dove into the golden slivers of delicious french fries.

On any day, in 8,000 McDonald's all across America, people eat millions of pounds of potatoes.

And around the world, in 3,000 more McDonald's, more millions of pounds of potatoes are gobbled up.

But that's only at the McDonald's chain. Still more potatoes disappear into hungry mouths in other fast-food restaurants: Burger King, Wendy's, White Castle, Arby's . . . Not to mention other, non-fast-food restaurants. And don't overlook the even vaster quantities of potatoes that you and hundreds of millions of other people eat at home.

Well, what about it?

Only this: That grubby little plant we call the potato is one of the four most important crops in the world. And it is about the most perfect source of nutrition so far discovered. Healthwise, the people of at least 130 countries would be badly off if suddenly they had to do without the potato.

Put a dollar sign on this vegetable. You come out with a staggering sum. The value of the potato worldwide is now $100 billion a year. If you were very rich, with an income of a million dollars a year, it would take you one hundred thousand years to earn that much money.

Where did the potato come from? How did it make its way into every corner of the planet Earth?

We'll see from the story of the potato's wanderings how something ordinary we hardly ever notice, like this lowly vegetable, can be just as important in the life of people everywhere as wars and revolutions, or kings and presidents.

A Strange, Funny-Looking Vegetable

One day in the 1530s a scouting party of Spaniards entered an Inca village, high in the Andes in what we now call Peru. Reports of cruel and greedy white invaders had already spread throughout the mountains, and the villagers had fled at word of their coming. The Spaniards went from empty house to empty house, hunting for loot. They found only maize (corn), beans, and a strange vegetable that was like nothing they had ever seen.

The vegetable came in many sizes, tiny as a nut to big as an apple. Its shape ranged from an irregular ball to a twisted oblong. Its skin was white, yellow, blue, purple, red, brown. Inside, its color could be white, yellow, purple, pink. The Spaniards were not impressed. They had come to the Andes searching for gold, silver, and precious stones. What good was this funny-looking vegetable?

Gradually they found out. First of all, it was the staple food of these mountain people. And secondly, the vegetable was believed to have healing powers. Raw slices were fixed to broken bones, pressed against the head to cure aching, eaten with other food to end a bellyache. The Incas also rubbed it on their bodies to cure skin diseases and carried slices to prevent rheumatism.

The Inca name for the vegetable was *papa*. It means tuber, a short, fleshy underground stem or root. The Inca gave other names to the many kinds of *papas* they grew. Those with red flesh they called "weep blood for the Inca." An especially hard kind was "knife breaker," and still others were "human-head" and "red mother." When the Spaniards tasted the potato, they found it delicious—"a dainty dish even for Spaniards," one conquistador admitted.

The diet of the common people of Peru was mainly vegetarian. True, some people fished along the coast or in the mountain waters of Lake Titicaca. Others occasionally hunted in groups, chasing down deer, wild llamas, bears, pumas, and foxes. Still others raised guinea pigs and ducks. But those were luxury foods. The main diet was maize and other vegetables in the lowlands. But in the highlands, where maize would not grow, it was the potato above all that people depended on. We now know that the native peoples living along the western coast of South America were growing and eating potatoes two thousand years before Columbus set sail.

They knew not only how to grow the potato but how to preserve it. After harvesting the crop, they spread the potatoes on the ground and left them overnight to freeze in the biting air of the high mountains. The next day the

> *The potato was not the only gift of the New World to the Old. Chocolate, peanuts, vanilla, the tomato, the pineapple, lima beans, red and green peppers, tapioca, the turkey—all enriched the diet of Europeans. The traffic in foods was not one-way. European colonists brought over vegetable seeds, wheat, chick-peas, sugarcane, barley, and the first cows. From Asia came bananas, rice, and citrus fruits, and from Africa, yams, cowpeas, coconuts, and coffee.*

men, women, and children assembled to stamp out the potatoes' moisture with their bare feet. They repeated this process for four or five days, until all the moisture was gone. What was left was a white potato flour that could be stored for years. The Inca name for what was probably the world's first freeze-dried food was *chuno*.

Scientists exploring the ancient tombs of the Inca have found evidence that *chuno* was bartered for other products. It was carried on the backs of llamas to the lower valleys and coastal towns, where it was exchanged for maize and manioc (another root food), clay pottery, and woven cloth.

When the Spaniards discovered the rich silver mines of Potosí (now in Bolivia) in 1545, they were quick to see the use of the potato, fresh or freeze dried, as food for the Inca they forced to work for them. It didn't take long for speculators in Spain to see a new way to get rich. They sailed across the Atlantic, bought up potatoes cheaply from the Inca farmers, and sold them at high prices to the native workers in the mines.

Here is a strange twist of history: The annual $100-billion value of the potato crop is three times greater than the value of all the gold and silver the Spanish lugged away from the Americas. The potatoes they took so lightly turned out to be worth far more than the gold and silver they killed for.

A Gift of the Inca People

*T*he potato was the most precious gift Peru gave to the world.

Over 3,000 years ago the native peoples of the Peruvian region migrated up into the Andes from the great forests of the east. In these new surroundings they had to reshape their life. The foods they were used to eating—manioc and maize—would not grow on mountains lofting miles into the cold skies. So these immigrants had to find other vegetables to eat. Somehow they discovered the wild tubers botanists call *Solanum*. That "somehow" conceals how marvelous the discovery was. Picture a people who have often seen a plant with hard little berries growing out of the gravelly ground. Everyone knows the berries are impossible to eat. Then one day, pulling up the plant, someone finds that below the ground are tubers and munches one; it tastes good. The people have discovered the vegetable that will end hunger for millions.

Slowly, patiently, learning from trial and error, the Andean Indians changed the wild tuber. It was bitter and tough-skinned, no bigger than a nut, when they began to work with it. But early on they learned to grow several types. Because the mountains and valleys of the Andes region vary greatly in climate and soil, the potatoes naturally vary too. And by the choices the Indians made of which tubers to cultivate, they could propagate special types of potatoes.

Among them was a hybrid that resists the frosty air. The farmers did not make the hybrids. They were the outcome of natural cross-fertilization. But it took great intelligence for them to select and plant the types that best met their own needs.

Then, as we have seen, they found a way to preserve the potatoes. So first by the discovery of the potato, then by the growing of frost-hardy types, and finally by preserving this food, the peoples of the region solved the problem of how to live at great heights. It's hard to imagine how anyone could have survived in the harsh mountain ranges of South America without the potato.

It was around 1200 B.C. that the first migrating tribes settled in Peru. Over the next two thousand years a series of great civilizations rose and fell. Then, beginning about A.D. 1100, the Inca clan and dynasty built the richest and most powerful society in the Americas. By the time of the Spanish conquest of Peru, the Inca empire was already 400 years old and stretched 2,000 miles along the western side of the continent. Within its boundaries lived about ten million people.

The empire was a dictatorship ruled by one man, the Inca, who controlled everyone's life. He and his family sat atop the government; then came the nobles, and way below them, the vast mass of peasants who were obliged to work for the state for a part of each year.

The Inca ruler was worshiped as a god. He held control of the empire by military power, with fortresses placed at key points, connected by a sophisticated network of mountain roads. While Inca culture was largely of the Stone Age, they were skilled workers in soft metals, and they used gold and silver freely for ornamentation (many of their temples were paneled in gold) and even for utensils. They wove artistic fabrics of cotton near the coast, and of llama and vicuna wool in the mountains. They had no writing, and used a kind of abacus of knotted cords to keep accounts. Their cities, notably the capital at Cuzco, were solidly built of stone.

While the Inca rulers and nobles lived in splendor, the peasants lived on the land in one-room stone huts with thatched roofs. They used niches in the wall for cupboards. They had no chairs or beds, but squatted on the earthen floor and slept on it, too, wrapped in big woolen blankets. Guinea pigs, which were raised for food, ran around the room, and a few llamas were kept outside within a stone fence.

The houses stood alone or grouped into small villages.

The Inca built their homes on rocky land, often halfway up a mountain slope, and saved the good land for farming. At the bottom, in the valley, the climate was hot or temperate. Above, near the top, was pastureland.

We've seen how the potato came to be the staple food of the mountain people. But to take a step further back in time, how did they learn to farm? And apply what they had learned to the cultivation of the potato?

No one knows exactly when farming began—in Peru or anywhere else. It's one of those human activities we take for granted, something people always did. Who would think of it as a rather recent invention? Yet it is, when you consider the long history of human beings on earth: about 2.5 million years. To think of that in easier numbers, let's say 2.5 million years is comparable to about one day—24 hours.

Archeological research tells us that farming has gone on for only about 12,000 years. Those 12,000 years, in our 24-hour comparison, are equal to only about 7 minutes in that day. Not very long!

Yet that tiny fraction of time has seen enormous changes in humankind's history. Those 7 minutes of farming made civilization possible. They freed people from having to wander everywhere in search of food. Before the invention of farming, people lived in tribes—families huddling together for safety in case they ran into enemies, human or animal. They got their food by hunting, fishing, and gathering wild plants. Most of the time primitive people were hungry, and they spent all their waking hours searching for food. Few of them ever reached the age of twenty-five.

Out of hunger, and curiosity too, they tried out the plants around them, sampling this leaf and that root, this berry and that seed. Their stomachs told them which made them sick and which made them feel good.

But it was millions of years before the prehistoric people learned how important seeds are. How could you know that if you put a seed into the earth, a plant would grow from it? Perhaps someone dropped some seeds by accident one fall and, the next spring, found some grain growing where the seeds had fallen. We will never know the precise moment when that great mental leap, connecting the two events, was first made, or by whom, or where. It happened, though, at last, probably in several places at about the same time; and it was the beginning of farming. People sowed seeds and took care of the plants until they could be eaten as food. The birth of the idea that would change the world happened some 12,000 years ago, or about 10,000 B.C.

You can see how farming led people to stop roaming around and to stay in one place. Here they grew their food, farmed, and raised livestock; began to live together

Before farming was invented, there were only about 3 million people on earth, or about the number now living in the city of Chicago. By 3000 B.C. the population had exploded to nearly 100 million. Farming meant more food, more food meant more people could be fed. And that meant more children lived to have children of their own. Today the world's population is over 5 billion.

in villages, towns, and cities; and thus created a civilization. The same process went on all over the world, for farmers did not always stay in one place. When they moved, they carried their food plants along. The movement of plants could go in any direction. When settlers came to the Americas after Columbus, they brought seeds of cabbages, beets, and turnips, as well as wheat and other grains. Later, inching from one coast to another of the Americas, pioneers took along the food plants they favored.

The potato, as we shall see, is one of the world's important plants that has experienced many migrations. It is a member of the genus of plants called *Solanum*—the

There are at least 20,000 edible plants in the world. About 3,000 have been used as food at some time or another. But only about 100 have been brought up to anything close to their potential, says Dr. Noel D. Vietmeyer of the National Academy of Sciences. The potato is one of them.

Latin word for nightshade. There are about a thousand kinds of nightshade, spread widely in temperate and tropical regions. This family includes, besides the potato, such plants as tomato, eggplant, pepper, bittersweet, petunia, and tobacco.

What part of a food plant do we eat? It varies. In corn, wheat, and rice, it's the seeds. In the potato, it's the thick parts of the underground stems—the tubers—that provide the food. The tubers grow from the tips of the plant's underground stem five to seven weeks after plant-

No, the sweet potato is not a potato. The true potato belongs to the nightshade family of plants; the sweet potato is a member of the morning glory family. Whether it's a potato or not, the sweet one is delicious when baked, mashed, or oven fried. China produces 80 percent of the world's sweet potatoes. Often the sweet potato is miscalled the yam. That's another form of vegetable, which comes as the yellow yam, white yam, winged yam, hard yam, or greater yam. Don't be confused!

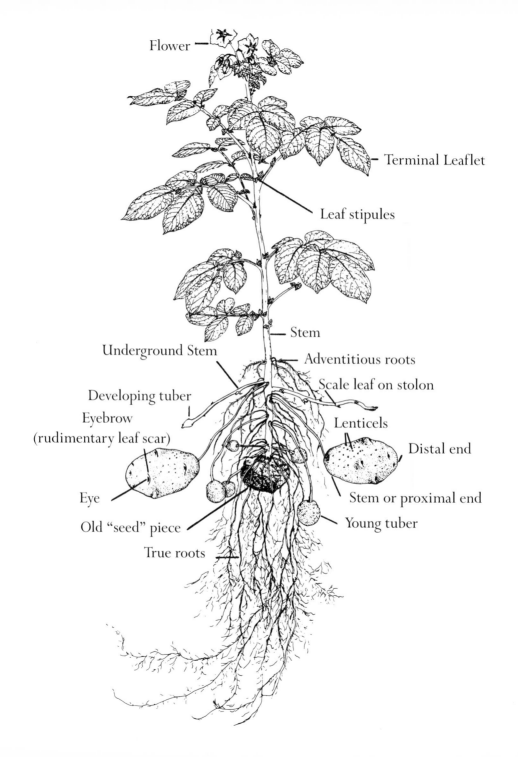

Flower

Terminal Leaflet

Leaf stipules

Stem

Underground Stem

Adventitious roots

Scale leaf on stolon

Developing tuber

Lenticels

Eyebrow
(rudimentary leaf scar)

Distal end

Eye

Stem or proximal end

Old "seed" piece

Young tuber

True roots

ing. At this time the plant above ground is six to eight inches tall, though this varies with the kind of potato and the surrounding conditions. As the plant grows, the green leaves make food for the plant's continuing growth. At some point a supply of this food is made beyond what the plant needs for growth. That extra food moves down into the underground tuber for storage.

What we call the "eyes" of the potato are really buds. New plants are started from pieces cut from the tubers, with at least one good bud or eye included in each piece. The starch in the piece feeds the young plant as it begins to grow.

How did the Inca grow their crops of potatoes? The farmers broke ground with a large digging stick, a sort of foot plow. It was driven into the soil by a thrust of the foot and the pressure on the handle. Then the long handle was pressed downward with a grip on the upper handle, and the clod of earth was forced up. The big clods of earth were chopped into small pieces by the

The various parts of the potato plant and the seed potato.

AGOSTO
CHACRAIAPVI

quilla

tienpo de labrança— hayllinmi ynca—

Above: An Indian in modern Bolivia using the foot plow, one of the most primitive agricultural tools

Left: Planting maize in Peru during the time of the Spanish conquest. The Inca men prepared holes in the ground with a foot plow and the women tossed in the seed.

women, who used stone-bladed hoes or wooden clubs.

Small groups worked side by side with their foot plows, keeping time by rhythmic chants. The aim of turning up the soil was to kill the coarse grass before planting the potato. The broken land was left for the winter. When sowing time came, the farmers dropped the seed tubers into the rotted grass of the turned-up soil. Farm labor generally was shared by men and women, but in some places in Peru the women did it all, while the men did the weaving and sewing.

THREE

Fear and Folklore

We know how the potato became a major food for the Inca. But how did the vegetable cross the Atlantic and arrive in the Old World? For a long time that story was more myth than fact. The truth is that as soon as the Spanish conquerors melted down the gold and silver objects of the Inca craftsmen, they shipped the loot home. And to feed the sailors on the long voyages, they packed potatoes aboard. That's how the plant reached Spain first, and then slowly spread throughout Europe.

But for about 250 years it was widely believed that the potato had come first to England, carried there from

Virginia. This mistake goes back to the famous English gardener John Gerard. A vain man, he prided himself on knowing more than anyone about plants, and especially the potato. In a catalog of plants in his gardens he made the first mention of the potato in print. A year later, in 1597 (the time when William Shakespeare was writing his earlier plays), Gerard claimed he had received the potato from what he thought was its native home in Virginia.

This was a simple error which involves the first Englishman to sail around the globe, Sir Francis Drake. On that first round-the-world tour, stopping at an island off the coast of Chile in 1577, Drake had been brought potatoes by the native people and learned what a useful food they were. Later, in 1586, on another voyage, Drake stopped at Cartagena in what is now Colombia and collected supplies, the potato among them, for his crew. On his way back to England he made a detour to pick up some starving English settlers who had had enough of Virginia and wanted to go back home. Understandably, it was assumed that the potatoes, along with the passengers, had come from Virginia. That error, like so many in history, was kept alive in book after book for a very long time.

The potato got off to a bad start in England. Queen Elizabeth I's cook, given the new plant, leaped to the wrong conclusion: He threw away the tubers and cooked the leaves. The Queen didn't like this new dish. Oddly, the potato did become a Virginia crop later, when Irish colonists carried it *back* across the Atlantic from Europe. England itself would not produce potatoes in any quantity until the late 1700s.

The Spanish, we know, were the first Europeans to speak favorably of the new vegetable and to enjoy the "dainty dish." In 1570 potatoes could be bought in the markets of Seville, and in 1573 they were being fed to hospital patients in other parts of Spain. One of Spain's historians, Bernabé Cobo (1653), not only told how to raise a potato crop but described how Spanish women used *chuno* to "make a flour more white and fine than that of wheat." From it, he wrote, "they make starch, sponge cakes, and delicacies with almonds and sugar

An artist's rendering of the type of Spanish ship that carried adventurers like Pizarro to the Americas.

added." And of cooked green potatoes "they make the most delicious fritters."

By the late 1500s potatoes were grown in Italy, then in Germany, Austria, and Switzerland, and finally in France. Tidbits from the early European beliefs about the potato come down to us in herbal books—guides to medicines made from herbs—of the 1600s. Doctors and apothecaries (pharmacists) learned valuable information about medicinal and other plants from these handbooks. But they also contained weird ideas: To herbs we know would have helped, the apothecary might be instructed to add a piece of toad, the juice of worms, the dried horn of a deer, and last but not least, animal droppings. Along with these tasty morsels a rich patient might benefit by adding a powdered pearl, ruby, or sapphire.

Herbalists played down the potato as food. Instead they stressed its merits for medicinal use. Carolus Clusius, a French botanist, reported that eating cooked potatoes was good for the health. While he warned that the vegetable could cause gassiness, he claimed that the potato "excites Venus"—that is, increases sexual desire.

Potatoes are sold at a vegetable market in the Netherlands in the 1600s. From a wood engraving by Jan van den Velde.

And more: It made for large families and a much longer life. One herbalist advised that a potato broth would cure diarrhea, consumption (tuberculosis), impotence in men, and barrenness in women.

On the other hand, some writers warned that eating too many potatoes would cause leprosy (perhaps because the twisted forms of some potatoes reminded people of how leprosy looked). And all over Europe the peasants feared the new plant would bring disease.

Why would people resist the potato? Because it was a new kind of food: Nothing like it had ever been seen in Europe. To eat it was not only a bold venture in diet but a radical break with the common tradition. And most powerful was the fact that the potato was not mentioned anywhere in the Bible. So if it was a food not designed for the people by God, how could they dare eat this evil thing?

What helped to change French minds about the potato was the experience of a pharmacist, Antoine Parmentier, in the Seven Years War. He learned to enjoy the potatoes fed him while being held a prisoner in Germany in 1757. To overcome the French fear of the vegetable, he invited famous people such as Benjamin Franklin to his home and fed them as many as twenty tasty dishes, all made with potatoes.

He also used a neat psychological trick to get French farmers to grow potatoes. He planted some in a sandy plot near Paris, during the day stationing guards around the potato patch. But at night he left it unguarded. What

plant could be so valuable? his neighbors wondered. Soon they began to steal the potatoes and plant them in their own gardens. As potatoes became the rage in France, Queen Marie Antoinette wore sparkling white potato blossoms in her hair, creating a new fashion for the women of Paris. Now France honors the ingenious Parmentier with potato dishes named after him. Today the famous cooking school L'École Rabelais requires students to prepare sixty potato dishes for graduation.

In 1744, Frederick II of Prussia had to command peasants to plant potatoes. He supplied them free and sent along soldiers to see that his orders were carried out. In 1764 a Swedish king ordered his people to grow potatoes.

Folklore and ancient customs gradually made room for the potato. When it was finally accepted, certain rituals long used during planting and harvesting time were

A miniature portrait of Queen Marie Antoinette, wife of Louis XVI of France, who decorated her hair with potato blossoms.

adapted to the potato, and the peasants practiced folk customs such as these:

- 🌸 *Carrying a dried potato in a pocket or suspended from the neck as sure protection against rheumatism.*
- 🌸 *Carrying a peeled potato in a pocket on the same side as an aching tooth, which would cure the tooth as soon as the potato crumbled.*
- 🌸 *Avoiding potatoes, especially at night, if you were a pregnant woman and didn't want your child to have a small head.*
- 🌸 *Laying the skin of a potato at the door of a girl on May 1 to show your contempt for her.*

Another reason the potato was slow to win common acceptance was the fact that it was taken up first by the aristocrats. In the 1600s it was royalty and the nobles who enjoyed it as a luxury. A century later, when the ruling classes wanted the working people to adopt the potato as their main food, the people begged off. No, they said, this luxury "isn't for the likes of us." That view

In an old English ballad of about 1700 we can hear the street cry of a woman carrying vegetables on her head:

Here's cucumbers spinnage and French beans
Come buy my nice sallery
Here's parsnips and fine leeks
Come buy my potatoes too.

About 100 years later, a collection of London Cries *pictures an Irish colleen pushing a barrow of potatoes through the town, crying:*

Potatoes, three pounds a penny, Potatoes
Augh fait, here's a kind-hearted lass of green Erin
Unruffled in mind, and for trifles not caring
Who, trundling her barrow, content in her state is
Still crying, three pounds for a penny, Potatoes.

had its reverse side: In the British Isles it was the poor Irish who first latched onto the potato; the English for a time felt it was degrading to eat a food fit only for the despised Irish peasants.

Then what finally did make the potato more acceptable to everyone? The commands of a king were much less important than broad social changes. A French historian who studied the issue writes: "In all places and at all times the potato has always arrived in the baggage carts of distress. . . ." He then cites the many wars and cereal-crop failures that ravaged Europe in the eighteenth century. When such disasters brought about hunger, the potato could save the day.

The potato was planted in poor regions at first, and spread from there to meet food shortages. Government officials soon realized how effective the new crop was. Given an equal surface of land to grow on, the potato crop could feed five times as many people as wheat. So for the poor farmer who held only a small bit of land, potatoes had great appeal. And when the wheat or rye crops failed, less harm was done to the community if potatoes were on hand.

"He's a cold potato," we say of some people. The expression comes from the fact that when a cooked potato gets cold, it loses the good earthy flavor it has when freshly cooked. You can make good use of leftover cold potatoes by blending them with a soup base. But who knows what to do with a person who's a cold potato?

"He dropped it like a hot potato." The newspapers will say it of a politician who takes a position on some issue—and then suddenly changes his mind when it proves unpopular.

Meanwhile, over much of Europe, the population was growing rapidly, for reasons not yet clear even today. Luckily, the potato crops were producing enough food to feed the increasing number of mouths. But drought had already damaged potato crops in some places. And in 1776 (the year of our Declaration of Independence) a strange new blight had ruined the potato crop in a corner of the Netherlands. By 1800 an official in a French province could see trouble ahead. He warned against relying on the potato alone. If grain crops were neglected and the potato crop should fail, he predicted, the people would suffer terribly.

The events we now call the Industrial Revolution played their part, too, in the increasing dependence upon the potato. The speed of industrial change varied from place to place. But new towns and cities sprang up everywhere to house the great numbers of people who came to work in the factories. Take one example, Manchester, England: 75,000 people in 1800, swollen to 400,000 fifty years later.

With the Industrial Revolution came mass poverty in the cities, for wages were very low. Working people rarely died of starvation itself, but bad living conditions took a terrible toll on life, especially on children. Hundreds of

THE POTATO-PEELER, *by the Dutch artist Vincent Van Gogh (1853–90). The potato, a cheap food for the Dutch peasants, figures in several of his early paintings.*

thousands died from diseases caught so easily in the overcrowded slums with their flimsy shacks, stinking air, and polluted water.

Most people at that time lived way below the minimum standard of nutrition set today. Meat was almost unknown on the tables of working people. The poor lived on bread, cheese, porridge, and potatoes. And for the very poorest—both in the city and on the farm—potatoes were the sole food.

In most places, says Professor R. N. Salaman, author of the monumental history of the potato, "the potato made no progress as a food of the people, until industrialists discovered that the easiest way to produce cheap goods, in order to capture the foreign market, was to pay the lowest living wage."

To the factory owners the potato seemed a heaven-sent gift. Their workers managed to survive on potatoes, the cheapest food on the market. So the industrialists could pay the lowest possible wage to keep alive the men, women, and children who did the work.

For that reason potatoes became the main or only food

in the country as well as the city. The landlords who owned large farms could decide to pay their agricultural labor very little, knowing they would get along on potatoes. A great many people survived on them.

But when the potato crop failed—a great many died, too. It happened in Ireland. . . .

FOUR

A Bridge Between Life and Death

Who introduced the potato to Ireland?

No one person, as far as we know. It probably happened by accident, back in 1588. A great fleet of ships, sent out by Spain to conquer England, was defeated by the English navy. Some of the Spanish ships, trying to sail home by going around the top of Scotland, were damaged by storms off the coast of Ireland. Their crews were killed or captured by the Irish, who took what they found on board—probably including potatoes. Some of those potatoes were planted along the Irish coast.

Methods of potato farming today are much as they have been for centuries.

Very soon the Irish of all ranks were eating potatoes. People everywhere began to think that Irish meant potato, in the same way they connect rice with China. Even today in the United States, the potato is mistakenly known as the Irish potato. How did it happen that the potato became the staple food of the Irish so quickly?

The story goes back to the twelfth century, to the day when Pope Adrian IV, the only English pope ever, gave control of Ireland to King Henry II of England. In the sixteenth century Irish revolts against British rule were savagely crushed by the soldiers of Queen Elizabeth I. The long war ended in the slaughter of more than half the population of Ireland and the destruction of the homes of great and small alike. The countryside, with its crops and cattle, was ruined.

Just as that terrible struggle ended, the potato reached the hands of the peasants. The chaos of the war helped open the way for the entry of the new food. The people were near starvation. So when the potato arrived, it met a desperate need. Sheer necessity overcame in a few years any resistance to a new food.

Here was a food easier to prepare than any before it. It could feed the family and the livestock and was cooked for both in the same iron cauldron on the open hearth. A diet of potatoes morning, noon, and night? Yes, for it offered the only chance of escaping the famine and disease that hammered at Irish doors. It was what kept the Irish alive, for though they did not know it, the potato is the most perfect natural source of nutrition so far discovered.

In the 1700s the population of Ireland grew with astonishing speed. By 1801, when the union of Ireland with Great Britain was forced by all-powerful England, the population had doubled, reaching nearly five million.

For nine tenths of the Irish the potato by then had largely displaced the old diet of meat, milk, and oatmeal. One acre could supply a family of six, even though an enormous amount—about ten pounds per person per day!—was eaten. The people came to depend more and more on the potato as the harsh British rule hemmed in their ability to make a living.

The cost of renting a potato patch, even on a bog, was

What's in that nutritional gold mine, the potato? The average potato of 150 grams has only 100 calories and provides the following vitamins and minerals: 50 percent of the U.S. RDA of vitamin C; 20 percent of vitamin B_6; 15 percent of iodine; 10 percent of niacin (a B-complex vitamin), iron, and copper; 8 percent of folacin (folic acid, another B vitamin), phosphorus, magnesium, and thiamin (vitamin B_1); 4 percent of zinc and pantothenic acid (another B vitamin); and 2 percent of riboflavin (vitamin B_2). Besides all these vitamins and minerals, it has potassium (750 mg.) and crude fiber (765 mg.). But it has no fat and is almost salt free, with a mere 5 mg. of sodium.

often outrageously high. Yet each family needed enough land to grow a supply of the food. The majority held little or no land of their own, except perhaps a tiny spot next to their home. On top of the rental—usually paid by labor for the benefit of absentee landlords—they had to give a portion of their potatoes to the Protestant Church of England, a tithe they bitterly resented.

The potato needed the least amount of cultivation of any crop. To prepare the ground, sow, and harvest the crop took, all told, only three months. So for much of his time the peasant had little to do and no way to earn money. One result: A great many men, women, and children roamed around in the summertime, when their own potatoes were gone, begging for money or for old potatoes on which to live. Drunkenness too became common. Denied elementary schooling, often kicked off the land for inability to pay rent, hanging on the edge of starvation, many of the Irish sank into apathy.

And still the population kept increasing. By 1840 it peaked at over eight million. Eviction from their homes became even more common for the peasants. Evicted people went begging or became squatters along the road, building shacks and growing their potatoes on scraps of land. Many committed small crimes to get themselves into prison, where at least they would be fed.

A British commission studied the situation of the Irish. "Their sufferings," the report said, were "greater than the people of any other country in Europe had to sustain."

That was the fatal year of 1845. Worse was around the corner.

FIVE

Famine in Ireland

As the summer of 1845 began, Ireland's potato crops were looking their best. Suddenly a change set in. First a dismal mist, then storms of rain and wind alternating with a vast and terrible stillness. In the fields farmers noticed brown spots spreading on the leaves of the potato plants, the blackened stalks slowly leaning over, the air heavy with the stink of decay.

In some farm districts there was only mild alarm at first. Potato disease was no stranger. But this proved different. Panic spread quickly as whole fields were laid waste in a few hours. Families who had gone to bed leaving green fields woke to find them blanketed in black.

Terrified by the sight, the people worked frantically, cutting the black stalks to stop the spread of the disease, setting fires to purify the air, piling turf and stones over the potato patches as though to bury the invader, sprinkling the fields with holy water, desperate to halt the demon devouring the land. But the blight swept over field after field, even invading barns and houses to capture stored potatoes.

"Where will Ireland be?" asked a frightened editor as the potato fields turned into a stinking mass. He knew only too well how dependent on this tuber was the very existence of an entire nation. For there had been many partial potato famines for the past hundred years. But none had ever been this bad.

The blight turned out to be an infestation by a new fungus—*Phytophthora infestans*. It was not a sickness of the potato itself but an invasion by a microscopic living organism, one that could and did reproduce itself at lightning speed. It had struck first in 1842 in North America, along the Atlantic coast, from Nova Scotia down to Boston. The fungus must have reached Europe in a diseased tuber carried in a ship.

It took some forty years before the disease was correctly identified and a treatment worked out. Meanwhile, many guesses as to the cause of the blight proved wrong, and the remedies proposed had no effect. The blight redoubled in 1846, preventing a new crop from being sown. In 1847 the disease let up, but it returned, full force, in 1848–1849.

It took five or six months after the potato crop's failure for famine to begin. By then every scrap of food, every

---

The late blight that ruined the Irish crops isn't the only enemy the potato has. Plant pathologists can tick off at least 46 fungal, 18 viral, 6 bacterial, and 5 worm diseases. Not to mention insects—especially the Colorado potato beetle, which happily feeds on luscious potato plants anywhere in the world. The job of the plant pathologist is to find some way to control such enemies.

piece of partly diseased potato that could be swallowed, was gone. In many districts the people began to starve. They ate anything, even rotted potatoes they knew had killed pigs and cattle. People slept in rags after they had pawned every scrap of clothing and their bedding too. As the blight hung on year after year, the grip of hunger tightened. When they could, people lived on blackberries, on cabbage leaves. In district after district they starved by the hundreds. Even if food had been available, they could not have bought it; they were penniless. Bands of starving Irish wandered the roads, begging for food, looking "more like famishing wolves than men," said one observer.

On one winter's day, wrote a visitor, he saw crowds of women and little children "scattered over the turnip fields like a flock of famishing crows, devouring the raw turnips, mothers half naked, shivering in the snow and sleet, uttering exclamations of despair while their children were screaming with hunger."

Two Englishmen traveled to Cork to see the district said to be hardest hit. They saw dead bodies lying on the

A view of the outside of a cabin providing sad shelter to a family devastated by the potato famine.

roadside. In some towns there were too many dead for them to bury. Everywhere, typhus was raging. Wherever they stopped, they were besieged by starving, almost naked beggars. They found deserted cabins, often with unburied corpses inside, and everywhere a spirit of hopelessness.

Tales of what happened in those anguished times have been handed down for generations. Families dug in the fields all day in the hope of finding enough potatoes for just one meal. A healthy seed potato was hidden away like gold for the next planting. Even a century later fathers would turn red with rage if a child wasted food. A farmer out plowing would not leave on the ground a single potato, however small, that his plow turned up. Old people, long after the famine, would burst into tears at the sight of a dish of potatoes, because they could never forget the time of starvation.

Was nothing done to help the starving?

Relief was up to the government in London. Private charities tried, especially the Quakers, but they could not

The world has suffered famine throughout history. In Egypt, from 1064 to 1072, the Nile failed to flood into the fields, to the ruin of farming. This caused a long famine. Too much rain spoiled the harvests in Europe in 1315–1317, and at least 10 percent of the population died of hunger. There were bad famines in the 1300s in both China and Russia. In the African countries of Ethiopia and the Sudan there were big famines in 1984–1985. It's estimated that about a million people died of hunger. Even now, in the 1990s, 500 million people throughout the world go to bed hungry every night. The reason: Poverty exists everywhere, and hunger is a result of poverty.

cope with so huge a problem. In the long run the British failed to meet the challenge. Public works were started to provide some jobs for the needy so they could earn the money to buy food. Food depots were set up and price-controlled meal from India was sold to those working on the projects. Soup kitchens handed out food free to the unemployed.

But it was never enough. Humane officials who really wanted to help relieve the suffering came up against violent opposition to government action by people who believed that government must never interfere with private enterprise. They opposed public aid to the poor, no matter how desperately it was needed.

Let's leave Ireland "to the operation of natural causes," said one high English official. Another, an advisor on economic affairs to the British government, said that he "feared that the famine in Ireland would not kill more than a million people, and that would scarcely be enough to do much good."

Much as the English may have despised the Irish, they were almost as brutal and harsh to their own poor. Today most people accept the responsibility of the government to step in and help people in a time of crisis. But

Emigrants leaving Ireland in 1874 from Queenstown Harbor, bound for New York.

what we believe now was not how government in the 1840s saw things. It took a long time for the new humanitarianism of that century to open people's hearts to the sufferings of others.

Back then, however, some coldly blamed the Irish themselves for their troubles and said they got what they deserved. Anyhow, it would all work out for the best in the end. The best? Ireland lost two million people because of the potato famine. One fourth of the total population. A million died of starvation and of diseases like cholera that struck when hunger weakened the body.

And a million more fled their homeland.

SIX

To America!
To America!

*T*he Irish potato famine caused boatloads of starving emigrants to flee to America. But they were not the first Irish to come. At least 100,000 had already entered the North American colonies before the American Revolution. In the early 1800s more came, seeking a better life and freedom from British rule.

When the blight devastated the potato crops, the stream of Irish entering American ports became a raging flood. Most of the Irish came penniless. Few had trades, industrial training or even elementary schooling. The only jobs open to them were unskilled and often tempo-

rary. Irishmen soon dominated jobs others did not want, jobs where cheap labor was hired by the day, such as construction work. The women worked mostly as domestic

A group of Irish household servants photographed in the early 1900s. For most Irish female immigrants, domestic work was the chief source of employment in America.

servants, putting in sixteen-hour days for as little as seventy-five cents a week plus board and room.

The very low wages paid the Irish forced large families,

sometimes two or three of them, into slum tenements, where living was a nightmare. Cleanliness, fresh air, and privacy were impossible. Cholera and other diseases thrived in such neighborhoods.

The most terrible price for living in an Irish immigrant slum was paid by the children. More than three out of five died under the age of five. The average age of Irish Catholics buried in Boston at that time was only thirteen.

Life was not made easier by the widespread prejudice against the Irish. People sneered at their nationality; mocked their customs, manners and speech; ridiculed their faith. They were feared, excluded, and persecuted (much as people everywhere fear and demean newcomers, strangers, outsiders). Anti-Irish feelings were openly expressed. "No Irish Need Apply" became an expected line in job listings.

In the 1840s towns in the northeast were full of Irish,

Irish squatters in New York's Central Park in the years before the 840 acres were developed into the public recreation area of today.

as canals were being dug and new railroad lines built. The old-time Yankees looked down on the immigrants as hardly members of the human race. The poor Irish, known as "Shanty Irish," were denied aid by the local charities. The government offered them no assistance or protection. Their homes were burned and their churches vandalized.

Emigration had promised to be an escape from poverty and hunger, but many fleeing the potato famine failed to reach safe harbor. Tens of thousands died at sea or soon after landing in America. Small wooden ships designed to carry lumber, not people, were widely used for years. Too old and unfit, they often sank in the stormy North Atlantic. In the famine year 1847, of 100,000 Irish who sailed, about 17,000 died at sea of epidemics carried aboard by passengers or crew. Another 20,000 died of disease soon after arrival in North America.

The enormous long-term impact of the potato blight on Ireland is hard to imagine. The Irish-American scholar Andrew Greeley explains it: "The Great Famine, for all practical purposes, destroyed Old Ireland. Emigration creamed off the surplus population and many, if not most, of the more gifted and talented younger generation. . . ." Between the years of famine and the Civil War millions of dollars were sent home by immigrants in America to bring relatives out. The young, the strong, and the enterprising left Ireland to enrich America.

The outflow to America continued long after the famine. In the 1890s alone nearly 400,000 Irish emigrated to the United States. And almost all stayed—only one out of twelve returned home. All together about 4.5 million Irish moved to the United States between 1820 and 1930. Another million went to other countries. Today 40 million Americans trace their ancestry to Ireland.

And what about the effects of the potato blight on America? It took a long struggle for the Irish to fulfill their hopes in America. But today they are considered among the most successful of ethnic groups. Measure them by education, income, influence, power, position—they are generally at or near the top.

In this pair of contrasting lithographs of 1854, an artist depicts (above) a famine-stricken Irishman on a Dublin wharf studying the announcement of sailings to New York, and (left) an Irishman who has prospered in America contemplating a return to his homeland.

SEVEN

The Answer to World Hunger?

*W*ay back in 1719 a colony of Irish immigrants settled at Londonderry, in the British colony of New Hampshire, and planted potatoes they had brought with them. That is how North America got the vegetable. But as in Europe, the potato was slow to win favor. So slow that master craftsmen would tell the apprentices they housed and fed: "You don't *have* to eat potatoes, we'll give you something else." For it was long the common belief here too that potatoes would make you sick and shorten your life.

Not until Thomas Jefferson championed it did the

potato make progress. After serving as American minister to France, he returned home in 1789 a lover of French cooking—especially of the *pommes frites* (french fries) he and Benjamin Franklin had so enjoyed in Paris. Jefferson liked to experiment with plants and tried his hand with the potato. Later, as President, he served potatoes at White House dinners, making them a fashionable dish.

Trouble arose in the early 1840s, when the blight struck American potatoes before it was carried to Ire-

Jefferson's pleasure in French cooking gradually spread. In The Carolina Housewife *of the pre-Civil War years, there is a recipe for "Charleston Potatoes à la Madame Genlis." She was an intimate of the French royal household. Her recipe for lyonnaise potatoes is probably the first notice of that dish in the United States. Soon after, many American menus included potatoes fried with onions in the manner of France's then second largest city, Lyons.*

land. By now the potato had won a place in American kitchens, and families raised them in their own gardens. But when the crop in New England turned into a blackened, stinking mass, horticulturists began to hunt for sturdier varieties. They were amateurs who loved gardening and were eager to develop new or better plants. One of these pioneers was Chauncey Goodrich, an upstate New York minister. He spent great amounts of time, energy, and money on potato experiments. But he lacked the knowledge of scientific methods of potato breeding needed to bring useful results.

Later, in the 1870s, Cyrus Pringle, a young Vermont farmer, acquired great skill in the technique of creating hybrids. His seeds produced varieties of potatoes that won international recognition. Other scientists too tried their hands at developing new, improved potatoes, and growers began raising the new varieties in many more parts of the country.

Science is able to create better and more varied kinds

A farmer gathers potatoes in Aroostook County, Maine.

of food through genetics, the branch of biology that deals with heredity and how related organisms vary as they evolve. Early genetic research showed results forty years after the fungal disease wiped out the Irish potato crops of the 1840s. A single wild species of potato was found that could provide resistance to the blight, and its genes were bred into other cultivated potatoes. That hybrid still remains the main weapon against *Phytophthora infestans*.

If science had only known how to achieve such a hybrid forty years earlier, there would have been no famine in Ireland. That country's history (and our own) might have been different in many ways. Plant breeders are now able to predict results when they cross-breed potatoes. By crossing wild potatoes with cultivated ones, they can produce new varieties that resist disease and insect pests better or grow well in spite of an unfavorable climate.

But hunger is still a terrible threat. The world's population, now over 5 billion, is increasing far faster than our ability to feed everyone properly, especially in the less-developed regions of our planet. By the year 2000

primula

farfalletta

Claudia

English majestic 50

Chioggia 40

bea

Naples round

Some of the many varied types of potatoes.

the world will have 7 billion people to feed. And the numbers will keep shooting up for at least thirty years more, while good farmland is not likely to increase.

What can be done about it?

The potato! That's the answer, say many scientists. Much of the leading research on the potato goes on at the International Potato Center (known as CIP, its Spanish acronym) in Peru, the plant's original home. The work is funded by governments, foundations, the World Bank, and the United Nations—all of them concerned about new ways to prevent famine.

The main job of CIP is to preserve the full genetic diversity of the potato. Why is this job so important? Because of what scientists call "genetic erosion," which affects many plant (and animal) species besides the potato.

Modern growers plant new varieties of high-yield crops for the market. These high-yield varieties often become the single varieties used worldwide, because they are so improved. However, improved is not perfect. New insect, virus, or fungus mutations or importations may

An enemy of the potato—the black-and-yellow-striped Colorado potato beetle—lights on a potato plant. The insect spread eastward from the Rocky Mountain region in the late 1850s, reached the Atlantic coast about fifteen years later, and soon invaded Europe as well, carried aboard ships.

unlock the genetic resistance of that single variety. If it is the only variety left, it means the chance of a widespread disaster, like that in Ireland in the 1840s, is greatly increased.

Another threat to maintaining genetic diversity (which really means simply the availability within a species of many different traits that can "mix and match" to create new strains and varieties) is the rapid deforestation that is destroying much of the world's valuable natural vegetation. When the world's home of a plant (or animal) species disappears, that species is not likely to survive, and a piece of the natural diversity of germ plasm is lost. This "stuff of life" contains the genetic code, shaped over millions of years in the wild state, that provides natural resistance and defense against disease and pests.

For such reasons CIP has rummaged through nature's pantry to collect 15,000 samples of native potato varieties from many countries in Latin America. Then, using a computer database, it sorted out duplicates to reduce the samples to about 5,000. It maintains these specimens in the field or in storage and protects them against

Terrorism offers a new threat to protection of the potato. The band of revolutionary guerrillas in Peru who call themselves "The Shining Path" attacked a busload of workers from the International Potato Center in 1988, killing a guard. A year later three storage buildings at the CIP experimental center were dynamited. The violence forced the scientific staff to move their work to Lima. The civil unrest that plagues Peru endangers the efforts of science to serve humanity.

weather and infection. For safety's sake CIP also has storage centers in two locations in other countries.

Why this powerful focus on the potato—a plant that for a long time most people mistakenly thought was an unhealthy food, full of fattening calories and starch?

First of all, because the potato provides nearly perfect nutrition. It's rich in twelve essential vitamins and minerals, especially in iron, magnesium, and vitamins B and C, and in complex carbohydrates, the body's best source of energy. It has better-quality protein than the soybean.

And it is 99.9 percent fat free. What's more, potatoes have the kind of fiber that helps to lower cholesterol. And so much potassium that they make even oranges envious. That's why heart experts put potatoes on the menu.

Second, the potato grows almost anywhere. And it yields more food energy per acre than grains do. If you plant an acre of potatoes, you'll get twice as much protein as from an acre of wheat. The potato also can avoid risks that grains cannot: Because it is a tuber crop, with the edible parts below ground, a storm will do it no harm.

Potatoes planted in temperate zones will usually take about 150 days to mature. But in warmer places they can be ready to harvest only 40 to 90 days after planting—a farmer in those climates can plant crops of potatoes in between slower-growing cereals such as wheat, rice, and corn.

With creative imagination CIP continues to apply its ingenious skills to the improvement of the potato. The plant is already the fourth most important food worldwide, after wheat, rice, and corn. As research improves

Circling the globe, the potato eventually won the praise of people everywhere. Here farmers in Kenya, in east Africa, bring in the potato crop in 1916.

and expands, the potato will provide an even larger share of the calories and essential nutrients the world needs.

The recent development of bioengineering can also help speed up progress. The old way of plant breeding demanded as much as twenty-five years of hard work

If you want to grow your own potatoes, it's easy to do. You can order good varieties of seed potatoes—Irish Cobbler, Red Pontiac, Red Gold are but a few—from commercial seed catalogs. The whole seed potatoes, not the sets of cut-up ones containing an eye or two, are best because they don't have to be sprayed with fungicide, and you can cut them into pieces with two or three eyes each. Cut pieces should be left to dry in a cool place for a few days before planting, so bacteria and fungi won't climb aboard the moist surfaces.

Some gardeners plant potatoes on the surface of the ground, mulching them with six to eight inches of hay or pine needles. Others plant them six to eight inches deep, about nine to twelve inches apart, in trenched rows thirty inches apart. As you see the sprouts come up, mound the soil around the plants. This keeps the light from penetrating any of the developing potatoes,

to introduce new genes—by cross-fertilization of many generations of adult plants, for example—into crops like the potato. Now, however, synthetic engineering can in-

which will turn them green and bitter.

Your plants will need lots of water as they form tubers. Don't let the potato patch dry out. Mulch the soil to keep them cool, and be sure to weed.

Large amounts of nitrogen are not needed. Just put a little compost around the plants when they are about a foot high, and feed the blooming plants with a weak solution of fish emulsion or some other nitrogen source.

You'll know the tubers are fully developed when the leaves die back. Leave the potatoes in the ground for a couple of weeks so they'll age. Then you can lift them out. Let them dry outdoors for a few hours, but not in direct sunlight, and store them in a cool, shaded place to prevent greening and sprouting.

All you have to do now is prepare them for eating in any one of the zillion ways cooks around the world have created.

troduce genes directly into the fertilized seeds to improve the potato's nutritional value and strengthen its resistance to pests and diseases—this, say the scientists, without any risk to those eating the new potatoes.

The potato's ability to fight off disease is especially important in the tropics, where high humidity and warm temperatures make the plants easier prey. So scientists seek to develop potatoes that will do well in places like Africa and Southeast Asia. China has now become the second largest grower of potatoes (Russia is now first) because the vegetable will feed, at low cost, the people who live in its vastly varied climate zones.

In North America just six varieties of potato yield 80 percent of the potato crop. And although potatoes are raised throughout the continent, a handful of states dominates the market. By far the biggest grower is Idaho. In 1987, that state's harvest was nearly 10 billion pounds. Washington came next at close to 7 billion, followed by Oregon, Maine, and North Dakota, each a bit above or below 2.5 billion pounds. Then came California, Minnesota, and Wisconsin.

What the whole country produces is 14.5 million *tons* per year. Sounds like a lot, but it's only 5 percent of the world's harvest—291 million tons.

Americans in 1990 ate 120 pounds of potatoes per person. Measured by weight, it was the fourth most important food in their diet.

If you want to see how potatoes are produced, you can visit one of the places famous for the crop: Aroostook County in Maine; Long Island in New York State; the Red River Valley of Minnesota and North Dakota; the Kaw Valley of Kansas; Bingham County in Idaho; and the San Joaquin Valley and Sacramento Valley of California.

Potato growing in the United States is always going on. There is not a single month in the year when potatoes are not being planted or harvested somewhere. They are harvested in Florida and southern California during the winter and early spring; in the Gulf and coastal states in late spring and early summer; and in the northern states in late summer and early fall.

EIGHT

Get 'em Easy,
Get 'em Quick

*I*t takes a mighty working force to grow America's potatoes and get them to the table. There are about 16,000 producers, packers, shippers, and processors of potatoes. The industry's first job is to get the best possible potato out of the ground to satisfy the consumers' tastes and needs. A grower may plant and harvest an entire crop to fill the special order of just one restaurant chain. The people who work at storage, packing, and shipping devise new ways to get the potato from the field to the table throughout the year.

Processing potatoes is a rapidly growing part of the in-

Harvesting red potatoes in Minnesota, one of the major growing states for the crop. Very little hand labor is used to dig, load, unload, wash, grade, and sack potatoes on large-scale farms.

dustry; it takes up half the annual U.S. harvest. The processor cleans, cuts, and/or cooks the potato in some particular way and packages it for home or restaurant use. Americans now eat more processed potatoes than the fresh kind.

Potatoes harvested in Idaho move along the conveyor belt to be checked for stones, dirt, and twigs before going to the storage area.

Women who work outside the home often no longer have time for old-style cooking. The more they clamor for "quick-preparation" convenience foods to ease their task, the more foods will come prewashed, prepeeled, precooked, premashed, premixed—almost preeaten! Ingenious ways to do these things to potatoes are dreamed up almost daily. They come dehydrated, frozen, and canned. You no longer have to peel and cook them. Just read the instructions on the package, use a bit of imagination, and you can put a variety of potato dishes on the table in no time.

With the enormous growth of the fast-food trade, America's old love affair with french fries reached new heights as the processors made them easier to prepare.

Have you ever been called a "couch potato"? Someone who stays glued to the TV screen and never takes exercise? Half the population are couch potatoes, according to one national study. And children especially. They use up more time watching TV than doing any other single thing except sleeping. Average two- to seventeen-year-olds devote upward of twenty-two hours each week staying with the tube. And while doing it they are likely to snack on potato chips. By the time today's child is seventy-something, he or she will have spent a full seven years in front of the TV.

Over five billion pounds of fries are eaten every year.

But food scientists point out what processing can do to the nutritious quality of the potato. Peeling a potato in the early stages of processing removes about half its fiber. Along the way, the vegetable also loses most of its vitamin C, for it is quickly destroyed by exposure to heat and air. French fries, potato chips, canned boiled potatoes, or dehydrated spuds may contain added fat and/or sodium. (Potatoes eaten fresh contain only a trace of fat and not enough sodium to mention.) Then too, some potatoes are packed with additives—to preserve, color, and flavor them—in the hope they will look and taste as good as when they were harvested. That kind of processing diminishes the quality of the processed potato.

Giving in to demand, major manufacturers of french fries are learning to fry with only polyunsaturated vegetable oils, which do not raise cholesterol levels.

Much of the money the big food companies put into research goes to develop processed foods and consumer appeal. In 1991 one could eat a nutritious food like the Idaho potato, direct from the field, for about 49 cents a pound. The more a potato gets processed, however, the more its price goes up and its nutritional value goes down. A package of frozen potato blintzes (13 oz.) was $2.59; scalloped potatoes, $2.19 for 11 oz.; and hash browns (17 oz.), $1.39. A bag of potato chips (6.5 oz.)

> *When you bite into something and it tastes like soap or Styrofoam, ugh! If food products are to be popular, they need to taste good. A big business has sprung up to overcome the loss of taste that may come from processing foods. With America growing more and more health conscious, food producers have reduced or cut out fat, sugar, and salt. To put back the tastes that are lost, experts engineer all sorts of flavors. Even the humble potato chip has been given a bouquet of flavors— oat-bran chips, mesquite chips, dill-pickle chips, crab chips, Cajun chips, to name a few. One flavor supply company has some 3,000 active flavors in racks of test tubes. The industry takes in over $2.5 billion worldwide.*

was $1.79. Each step in processing offers a new chance for more profit.

It's worth noting that many of the methods used in processing food were developed with public funds, according to a Federal Trade Commission study. The public's tax dollars bought research that went into frozen concentrated juices, prepared mixes, low-calorie foods and drinks, baby foods, dried milk products, instant beverages, frozen poultry, and refrigerated biscuits.

Today, food processing plays a big role in spreading American-style eating around the world. In Moscow, for instance, a McDonald's complete with french fries made from Russian potatoes has proven a great success.

A Delicious Dish—
In Any Language

"The world's ways with the poor man's food and the gourmet's delight are endless," say Maria and Jack Scott, famous cookbook authors. And to prove their boast about the potato they remind us that Americans:

have created more stuffings than anyone, blending the mealy baker with everything from cottage cheese to caviar and salmon. We also hash, mash, mince, fry, steam, boil and roast them; add them to improve soups and chowders; combine them with cheese, onions, butter and milk as a main dish, team them with tuna, couple them with chicken, make croquettes, pair them with leftover meat in a pie, create unique casseroles, put them in stews, pat them into patties, even make delicious doughnuts and chocolate cake with them.

And what about the winning ways of other nations with the lowly potato? The Scotts continue:

The French who fondly call the potato *pomme de terre*, "apple of the earth," do much more than French fry potatoes. They have over 100 classic recipes, from the dramatic *pommes de terre soufflées*, which puff into hollow golden balls, to the impressive *pommes Anna*, potatoes sliced very thin, baked in sweet butter and turned out like a cake.

The Germans, who may respect the potato most, . . . use it for noodles, dumplings, pancakes and bread. They imaginatively mix mashed potatoes with apple-sauce, sugar and vinegar, use potatoes to stuff geese and make a renowned hot potato salad.

In Russia and Poland, the potato . . . is the base for many soups. It is stewed in sour cream; patties are

Potato dishes, ready to serve.

For weight worriers this chart compares potato calories with 15 other foods we eat or drink.

	calories
Potatoes——boiled, 1/2 cup	45
mashed, milk added	70
baked, 1/2 cup (1 medium)	90
potato salad with dressing, 1/2 cup	99
Spaghetti, cooked——3/4 cup	115
Bread——2 slices	120
Biscuit——1	130
Candy——1-oz. chocolate bar	150

stuffed with spicy mushrooms, and both countries make famous potato puddings and ingeniously stuff the vegetable with meat and fish.

The Italians turn the *patate* into their famous *gnocchi*. The Spanish fill a spectacular omelet with *papas*, the Greeks make a superb sauce, *skordalia*, with

Rice, cooked—3/4 cup	*150*
Sweet potato, baked—1 medium	*155*
Milk, whole—8 oz.	*165*
Peanuts, roasted—1 oz.	*170*
Pancakes—3 or 4 in. diameter	*180*
Pizza—1/8 of 14-inch pie	*180*
Macaroni with cheese—1/2 cup	*240*
Ground beef—3-oz. patty	*245*
Steak—4 inches x 2 1/2 inches x 1/2 inch	*330*
Cake, chocolate—2-in. section of 1-in. sheet cake	*420*
Milkshake—12 oz.	*520*

potato, olive oil, garlic and lemon, which they serve with seafood, and the Swiss have created *roesti*, a flat potato cake that has become the national dish.

If you're cooking potatoes at home, what advice do the experts offer? First, there are the two basic types, called waxy and floury. The waxy are quite low in starch and stay firm when cooked. Best to use them for boiling and steaming. The floury ones are starchier and, when cooked, fluffy in texture. People use them for baking, mashing, frying and oven frying, and gratins. The best-known starchy variety is the Idaho Russet. It's grown in that state's volcanic soil and is a great favorite.

Out shopping, don't buy potatoes that are bruised, flabby, cracked, or spotted green. You want them fairly clean, firm, and smooth, and with a regular shape so there won't be too much waste if peeled. If you plan to bake several at the same time, they should be roughly the same size so they'll take the same amount of time to be done. It's best to pick them out one by one rather than buying them by the bag; that way you can inspect each. When you store them, keep them in a dark, dry place, loosely covered and unwashed. Don't refrigerate them, because cold turns the starch to sugars. And warmth makes them sprout and wither.

Here are some tips on how to prepare your potatoes for cooking:

🌢 *To clean potatoes, gently scrub them with a vegetable brush or cellulose sponge.*

🌢 *To conserve their nutrients, leave the skin on the potatoes during cooking.*

🌢 *If you must peel potatoes before cooking them, use a vegetable parer, keeping the peelings as thin as possible, since some of the nutrients are stored close to the skin.*

🌢 *Although potatoes keep nutrients better when cooked whole, if you're in a hurry, you can halve, slice, or dice them before cooking. Make the pieces the same size so they'll cook evenly.*

🌢 *If you don't cook them right away, peeled potatoes turn dark. To hold their whiteness, toss them with a little lemon juice.*

Remember: Prolonged soaking of potatoes in cold water can result in some loss of vitamins.

The number and variety of recipes using potatoes are staggering. Hundreds of new cookbooks are published yearly, and almost every one of them contains potato recipes. *The Great Potato Cookbook* by Maria Luisa Scott and Jack Denton Scott has over 350 recipes, while Sue Kreitzman's *Potatoes* contains 68 recipes, and J. McNair's

Potato Cookbook has 35. They range from soups and knishes to hearty stews and delectable desserts. I learned that not only are there potato cakes, pies, doughnuts, cookies, and candies, but that some are made with chocolate, too! Truffles, tortes, and patés combine potatoes with chocolate. There is even a chocolate ice cream based on potatoes so that potato-fanatic chocoholics can enjoy both favorites with each lick or bite.

More and more, the once-lowly potato is carried to new culinary heights. A simple baked potato is always good, and so is the boiled potato with parsley. But chefs seized by flights of fancy cater to people's desire for the familiar—with a twist. One of them takes pasta dishes and does them with potatoes instead. He wraps sheets of potatoes around salmon and basil and calls it cannelloni. He makes ravioli out of potatoes and oysters, lasagna out of potatoes layered with wild mushrooms and chives drenched with truffle sauce.

You may call such dishes gimmicky, says one chef, "but the potato is so versatile; almost anything you put with it will work." And why not? Potatoes, notes one food editor, "are emotional, basic, elemental. They are, more than any other food, an object to be elevated, re-created and redesigned."

Bibliography

A Note on Sources

Index

✿ *Bibliography* ✿

American Potato Journal, Supplement, Vol. 57, 1980.

Braudel, Fernand. *Capitalism and Material Life*. New York: Harper, 1973.

Brody, Jane. "As Its Virtues Emerge, the Potato Goes Global." *The New York Times*, October 9, 1990.

Brown, Elizabeth Burton. *Vegetables: An Illustrated History with Recipes*. Englewood Cliffs, NJ: Prentice-Hall, 1981.

Coogan, Timothy. *Ireland Since the Rising*. New York: Praeger, 1966.

Cummings, Richard O. *The American and His Food*. New York: Arno, 1970.

Daniels, Roger. *Coming to America: A History of Immigration and Ethnicity in American Life*. New York: Harper, 1990.

Dodge, Bertha S. *Potatoes and People*. Boston: Little, Brown, 1970.

The Economist. "Let the Sky Rain Potatoes." October 13, 1990.

Edwards, R. Dudley, and T. Desmond Williams, eds. *The Great Famine: Studies in Irish History, 1845–52.* New York: New York University Press, 1957.

Fenton, Carroll Lane, and Hermine B. Kitchen. *Plants We Live On.* New York: John Day, 1971.

Forster, Robert, and Orest Ranum, eds. *Food and Drink in History.* Baltimore: Johns Hopkins University Press, 1979.

Foster, R. F. *Modern Ireland: 1600–1972.* New York: Penguin, 1989.

Greeley, Andrew M. *The Irish Americans: The Rise to Money and Power.* New York: Harper, 1981.

Jones, Evan. *American Food: The Gastronomic Story.* New York: Dutton, 1975.

Kreitzman, Sue. *Potatoes: 68 Delicious Recipes for Everyone's Favorite Vegetable.* New York: Harmony, 1989.

Lappé, Frances Moore, and Joseph Collins. *Food First: Beyond the Myth of Scarcity.* New York: Ballantine, 1979.

Marcus, Steven. *Representations: Essays on Literature and Society.* New York: Random House, 1975.

Marrin, Albert. *Inca and Spaniard: Pizarro and the Conquest of Peru.* New York: Atheneum, 1989.

Métraux, Alfred. *The History of the Incas.* New York: Schocken, 1969.

Morris, Richard. *Evolution and Human Nature.* New York: Putnam, 1983.

Parry, J.H. *The Age of Reconnaissance: Discovery, Exploration, and Settlement, 1450–1650.* Berkeley, CA: University of California, 1981.

Powledge, Fred. *Fat of the Land*. New York: Simon & Schuster, 1984.

Rhoades, Robert E. "The World's Food Supply at Risk." *National Geographic*, April 1991.

Root, Waverly, and Richard De Rochemont. *Eating in America: A History*. New York: Morrow, 1976.

Salaman, Redcliffe. *The History and Social Influence of the Potato*, rev. ed. London: Cambridge University, 1985.

Scott, Maria Luisa, and Jack Denton Scott. *The Great Potato Cookbook*. New York: Bantam, 1980.

Sokolov, Raymond. "The Peripatetic Potato." *Natural History*, March 1990.

Tannahill, Reay. *Food in History*. New York: Stein & Day, 1973.

Turnquist, Orrin C. "A Few Rows of Garden Potatoes." *Yearbook of Agriculture*, 1977.

Wolf, Eric R. *Europe and the People Without History*. Berkeley, CA: University of California, 1982.

Woodham-Smith, Cecil. *The Great Hunger*. New York: Signet, 1964.

✺ *A Note on Sources* ✺

Salaman's book is the most comprehensive source for the history of the potato and its significance in almost all times and places. A work of immense scholarship, and very readable, it is probably too detailed for all but the most avid students of the subject. The reader can assume Salaman was a major source for all but the last chapter of this book, so I will not list him chapter by chapter.

INTRODUCTION:

The facts about fast-food eateries and the volume of potato sales are taken chiefly from reports in the food and business sections of *The New York Times*.

CHAPTERS 1 and 2:

Métraux and Marrin give compact portraits of Inca life and the invasion of the Spaniards. Brown discusses findings of archeologists in the Andes that reveal the development of their agriculture and the cultivation of the potato. Dodge, Tannahill, the Scotts, and Wolf provided background on the evolution of farming. A special publication of the U.S. Department of Agriculture was devoted to this subject, using many graphic devices to bring it home especially to young readers.

CHAPTER 3:

French historians Forster and Ranum edited a collection of scholarly articles from the innovative French journal called *Annales*. Its aim is to cut across many fields of sciences, both the natural and social, to bring together the life of ordinary people and their everyday problems. I drew on their introduction and on the article "The Potato in the 18th Century," by Michel Morineau. Braudel (a founder of the *Annales* school of history) contains a great many insights on the rise of the Industrial Revolution and its effects on daily life.

CHAPTERS 4 and 5:

Coming to Ireland, I must point out that Salaman gives more than 150 pages to the introduction of the potato in that country and its complex social, economic, and political consequences. The other major sources here are Coogan, Edwards, Foster, and Woodham-Smith, whose vivid and harrowing portrayal of Ireland's "Great Hunger" was a best-seller when it appeared. The chapter in Marcus called "Hunger and Ideology" is a searing analysis of how rigid thinking (in this case, the economic theory of Victorian England) can bring about monstrous social injustice.

CHAPTER 6:

Greeley—the Irish-Catholic priest who is a popular novelist as well as a sociologist—is excellent on the Irish immigration to America and the course of Irish-American life since that time. Daniels is a new study of immigration history of all ethnic groups, which offers the results of the most recent research on the Irish.

CHAPTERS 7 and 8:

Dodge has many details on the early-nineteenth-century horticulturists and their work with the potato. Brody, *The
Economist*, Rhoades, Sokolov, and publications of the International Potato Center in Peru also provided data. Figures on
potato production come from the U.S. Department of Agriculture's *Agricultural Statistics 1989* and from the 1989 *Information Please Almanac*. Facts on the potato industry in America
are from publications of the National Potato Council in Colorado. The medical view of the processing of potatoes is
found in the *Tufts University Diet and Nutrition Letter*, July 1990,
and the economic view in Lappé and Collins.

CHAPTER 9:

For information on potato dishes and their preparation I re-
lied on books about food, eating, and cooking—Brown, Cummings, Forster and Ranum, Jones, Kreitzman, Root and De
Rochemont, and the Scotts. I also riffled the pages of the row
of cookbooks in our kitchen, just to get an idea of how indis-
pensable the potato is to any cook, amateur or professional. If
you want to try some potato recipes yourself and have no

cookbooks at home, any school library or bookstore is sure to offer plenty of choices.

<hr/>

Special thanks are owed to Ron Walsh of the National Potato Council and R. G. Webb of the U.S. Department of Agriculture's research staff. They replied promptly to my appeals for information. Encouraging at the very beginning of this project was Professor Rudolf Schmid, of the Department of Integrative Biology, University of California at Berkeley. He also provided a reprint of his article on some recent botany books for children and young adults (*Journal of the International Association for Plant Taxonomy*, February 1990; the article appeared in a revised version in the spring 1990 issue of *Appraisal*). I think all writers, illustrators, and editors of children's books in this field would find it useful.

Finally, I must thank once more my warm friend Anne Grandinetti, who for more than thirty years has managed to put into coherent typescript my scrawled-over drafts.

Index

Page numbers in *italics* refer to illustrations

❧ *About the Author* ❧

Milton Meltzer has written over eighty books in the fields of history, biography, and social reform. His series on American ethnic groups includes *The Chinese Americans*; *The Hispanic Americans*; and *The Jewish Americans*, which was an ALA Notable Children's Book. His highly acclaimed *The Black Americans: A History in Their Own Words*, also an ALA Notable Children's Book, was revised and updated in a single-volume edition. He also edited *The American Revolutionaries: A History in Their Own Words 1750–1800* and *Voices from the Civil War: A Documentary History of the Great American Conflict*, both named on "best book" lists. His two books on the Holocaust—*Never to Forget: The Jews of the Holocaust* and *Rescue: The Story of How Gentiles Saved Jews in the Holocaust*—are widely used in Holocaust studies and are now available in paperback.

His many other honors include five nominations for the National Book Award, most recently for *All Times, All Peoples: A World History of Slavery*, which also won the Christopher Award. Another title for Harper, *Ain't Gonna Study War No More: The Story of America's Peace Seekers*, was an ALA Notable Children's Book, an ALA Best Book for Young Adults, and the recipient of the Jane Addams Children's Book Award.

His most recent book is *The Bill of Rights: How We Got It and What It Means*.

Mr. Meltzer was born in Worcester, Massachusetts, and educated at Columbia University. He lives with his wife in New York City. They have two daughters and two grandsons.

635
MEL

Meltzer, Milton

The amazing potato

M28066

$14.89

DATE			